GROUNDWORK

Amanda Jernigan

GROUNDWORK

poems

with wood engravings by John Haney

BIBLIOASIS

FIRST EDITION

Library and Archives Canada Cataloguing in Publication

Jernigan, Amanda, 1978-
    Groundwork / Amanda Jernigan.

Poems.
ISBN 978-1-926845-25-8

    I. Title.

PS8619.E75G76 2011   C811'.6   C2011-903499-9

The cover is after John Haney's photograph *Island 94*.

Readied for the Press by Eric Ormsby.

 Canada Council   Conseil des Arts
for the Arts   du Canada

 Canadian   Patrimoine
Heritage   canadien

 ONTARIO ARTS COUNCIL
CONSEIL DES ARTS DE L'ONTARIO

Biblioasis acknowledges the ongoing financial support of the Government of Canada through the Canada Council for the Arts, Canadian Heritage, the Canada Book Fund; and the Government of Ontario through the Ontario Arts Council.

PRINTED AND BOUND IN CANADA

for John

You bolted the frame of my loom to your deck
so that I can weave in all weathers,
and carved me a shuttle of olive wood.

You warp the loom in rain-fine thread,
and weave without unravelling
the winedark tapestry through which we tack.

POEMS

WOOD ENGRAVINGS

EXCAVATIONS

The Night Guard

The cattle have been banished from the field.
You've shovelled up the topsoil, with its freight
of pottery and dung, and wheelbarrowed it away
to the northwest corner. You've trowelled back
the later strata, Islamic and Byzantine,
at last laid bare the structure of your thinking.

Like whistling boys, the hours of the night
harass the moon. A cat moves in the cacti.
One of her ears has been chewed off, her tail's
gone tatty. She'll leave her footprints in the trench
before night's through. I watch the stars draw in
like eyes. The ruins outface them, wait for you.

The Fieldworker

The sky will hold its dark for an hour yet.
The street lamps glare, wild orange eyes.
At the edge of town, the avenues forget
themselves, lapse into gravel. At the site,
we start by sweeping trenches: by first light,
above the field, slow clouds of dust will rise.

The sky becomes a great blue gong
struck by the sun each hour. Now I loan
my limbs to work – but later, in the long
hot noon, I'll ponder the mind that made
an aegis of an oxhide, in the shade
of courtyards walled by ranks of pillaged stone.

At nightfall I will nurse my Tuareg tea,
and watch the lights of Tunis, alter ego
of the Punic town. From neither land nor sea
arrived the force that wrecked the Punic queen:
the sly worm in the heart contrived to drain
the flask from inside. *Delenda est Carthago.*

We've found a wealth of marble on this site.
Each piece is scrubbed and polished up, for show,
then sorted, serpentine from hematite.
Once the stone is classified, it's lumped
on scales, the weight recorded; then it's dumped,
out where the chickens scratch and the cacti grow.

The Scholar

The third floor of the library is home
to classics, history, the outsize art.
A dozen years of study. Now these stacks
comprise the whole *urbs urbis* of my heart.

Outside, the wind, unhurried, sculpts the drifts.
Inside I read of deserts, sand-stormed towns,
an army forced to march in place all night –
by dawn, the palms were buried to their crowns.

If snow is sand's translation, 'sculpt' won't do
for this entombing wind – for sculptors hone
the negative imagination, look
to see Laocoön within the stone.

An archaeologist does much the same.
The books and maps, whatever is to hand,
will help, but in the end I must project
this ruin, think it deep within the sand

until it's reached arboreal perfection.
I think sometimes of Schliemann, what he found
at Hisarlık by conjuring with Homer,
producing Troys, like rabbits, from the mound.

Nine Troys all told – which is to say nine gates
of fire, nine times walls reduced to rubble,
nine times people slaughtered in their homes.
Of course. We dig the artifacts of trouble.

They say this floor is haunted. Once I watched
as each great shelf came crashing down, one stack
upon the next. Beneath each Troy there is
another. How is one to put them back?

The Smuggler

'Permit me but these tesserae,' I said
to the overzealous customs guard. 'Disturbed
stratigraphy yields nothing to the Bardo;
the mosaic these belonged to long ago
was smashed by Vandals, or lifted by collectors,
or rucked up by the farmer's hoe. I want
to sow these dragon's teeth.'

                         He said, 'Strange crops
will grow. I must require of you these seeds.'
I fumbled with my pack, to stall. He sent me
to the tail end of the queue.

                         When I approached
the desk again I took a different tack:
'I've seen the apocalyptic aunties, stooped
above a table in the sky. They are
assembling a puzzle. At the end of time,
they'll fumble for their glasses – I'll confess
to having pocketed these three, and place
the final pieces.'

                      But he scowled. I knew
the image wasn't apt. A mosaic is
a work of art, and that's no jigsaw. I watched
a granny handling a luggage cart
piled high with bags, some children ducking
the cordon rope. The speaker summoned me,
not for the first time, to the gate.

                         When I
approached the desk again I had my answer
ready: 'Listen. I'll be frank with you.
When the archaeological angels come, in Munsell
colours, silt and humus raining from

their wings, how shall they know me? Let me keep
these for a sign.'

                       'I know those angels,' said
the guard. 'Most powerful of all is Dust.
They call her Mnemosyne. You do not want her
to remember you.' He stripped me of my tesserae.
A shame. I should have liked to question them
about the nature of the picture. I suppose
they would be mute as dice.

I boarded with empty pockets once again.

The Physical Anthropologist

Death was patient with the three bright-robed patricians,
patrons, maybe, of this church, who were buried beneath
the adamant mosaic. Patient, also, with the thieves,
who scattered the golden tesserae to loot the tomb,
a century later, and found the bones, diminished things:
the little men behind the curtain. Death will be likewise patient
with the scholars, who fall to sweeping in the morning light.

Slow clouds of dust rise above the field. Breathe deeply.
If you walk a few miles up the road, you'll find a hill:
a hummock, really. This marks the walls of ancient Carthage.
There's little left. The living have quarried the bricks of the dead.
And why not? When the scholars leave, La Marsa men
will plant tomatoes in the font. Their arms are bare,
the fruit so round and brazen all my learning can't articulate.

The Cartographer

In the mountains to the west
there are wonders water-made.
All the slopes are green-inlaid.
There the giant takes his rest.

Let us follow any stream
until it's lost itself in sand
to find the unforgetting land
that we may excavate his dream.

First the men who moved like motes
across the desert, travelling
to strange reunions, ravelling
their caravans; then men in boats,

who opened harbours in his side
that skiffs and biremes might admire
their reflections, men from Tyre;
then he dreamed a Roman tide.

thrice the ebb and thrice the flow
before the overwhelming. The Romans
called the land accursed, but omens
pale – they soon returned to plow.

He then dreamed men of piety,
each bearing in a jewelled box,
which is to say a church or mosque,
another perfect deity.

Now, in the shade of the medina,
vendors hawk whatever sells.
A litter of copper bracelets, bells,
Nintendo sets and painted china:

an archaeologist's refrain.
Above us in the potsherd sky
no cumulus perturbs the eye,
but in the mountains there is rain,

and things do not stay buried there.
Who among us will be found,
and in what postures, overground,
when Atlas excavates the air?

The Cook

Get the cook with the frying pan!
The goat has got in the trench again,
and butted the buttresses, and stamped
the tesserae to dusty wine.

How many scholars – I'll be sworn,
the *nerve*, at this ungodly morning
hour, to rouse me – does it take
to take a bolting she-goat by the horns?

They swear their dusty faces blue.
I've yet to see a one eschew
a bit of chèvre with his lunch,
my signature goat's-cheese ragout.

The Photographer

All day I watched the archaeologists expose
their finds: terra cotta lanterns; Roman
coins; a Corinthian column capital found
intact; fists full of tesserae, some bearing
still the traces of their gilding, like broken
teeth; and broken teeth, for all I know.
Out of the filled-in cistern they took
your marble hand, its gesture unmistakable,
the reason for it long since lost. I'll bury
it again in the small night of my camera.

FIRST PRINCIPALS

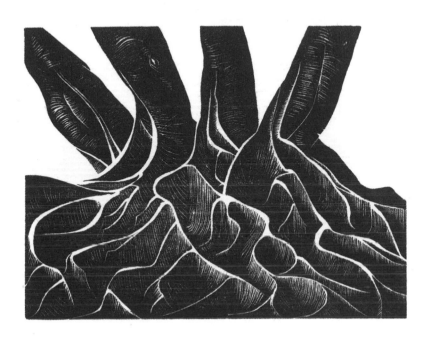

Aubade

The time, if time it was, would ripen
in its own sweet time. One thought of dawn.
One felt that things were shaping up,
somehow, that it was getting on.

Day broke. Upon the waters broke
in waves on waves unbreaking and
night fell, unveiling in its wake
one perfect whitened rib of land.

I slept, and while I slept I dreamed,
a breaking wave, a flowering tree,
and all of one accord I seemed.
I woke, and you divided me.

Adam's Prayer

In the sweat of thy face shalt thou eat bread:
you put this rather beautifully,
and gave me leave to sing my work
until my work became the song.

In sorrow shalt thou eat of it:
a line on which a man might ring
the changes as he tills the ground
from which he was taken. Thistle, thorn

(in the which is the fruit of a tree yielding seed),
these too shall it bring forth to thee,
all the days of thy life till the end,
the synagogue of the ear of corn.

Poem and plowman cleave the dark.
One can't eat art. But dust is art,
and unto dust shall I return.
O let my song become my work.

The Birds of Paradise

Adam and Eve and Pinchme
went down to the river to bathe.
Adam and Eve were drowned.
Who do you think was saved?

Between her pills, his poisons,
the water in which we bathe
is less than pure: I rather doubt
that even I'll be saved.

My pet canary, William, died.
But, I am reassured,
there is a factory upstream
to replicate the bird

in polyvinyl chloride: moving
parts, a voice-box *cheep* –
with proven nightingalish means
of putting one to sleep.

Do I wake or sleep? Indeed,
the answer is the same.
Ask Finnegan. In fact, ask me,
if you can guess my name.

Exodus

All the names ran out of my mouth like animals.
I couldn't find them when I looked for them. I called –
they wouldn't answer to themselves. I was reduced
to laying traps, to setting snares. And even
when a quick brown fox had kicked its last in my clever
knots, even then, especially then, the words escaped me.

Lowly

Lowly I am, though highly born.
Many a jewelled cloak have worn;
many a jewelled cloak have lost,
and left it to lie where it fell in the dust

and the underbrush. No man may tell
whether I augur head or tail.
In the morning when the world began
I went on four legs. Now I have none.

Off-Season

I rest the sword across my knees
and lean against the garden gate.
I check my pocket for the keys.
The trees are heavy with their fruit.

You may discern, at orchard's end,
by what scant light the moon affords,
two meagre figures, hand in hand,
diminishing horizonwards.

Peopled, Eden was, it's true,
a pleasant park in which to ramble;
I myself once found it so.
But empty it's a better symbol.

Soliloquy

All make-believe amounting to pretending
to the throne, I banished Eve, and Adam,
loath to go it on his own, went after.
That year the grapes fermented on the vine,
the fields lay fallow. I thought I'd take a stab
at beekeeping, but years have passed: you almost
wouldn't know there was a garden here. The streams,
uninterrupted, flow from Eden as they always did.
The apple trees, untended, go to crab.

Four Rivers Flow from Eden

One bears the tears of Eve.
It offers up the summer fruit,
reflected, to the summer tree
that gets down on its knees to see
branch ramified as root.

One bears the words of Adam,
and with its current swims
the fish of the sea after his kind:
haddock and char, downstream to find
the nets cast for their names.

One bears the voice of God,
dividing land from land.
It juggles suns: first one, then two,
then three, a million! hallelujah –
spills them in the sand.

Four rivers flow from Eden,
and all of them are true
and all flow from a single source,
but one meanders in its course.
It ravels like a clew.

Delivery

The *News* has been delivered: worse and worse.
I leave it open for you on the table and go out.
A pair of migrant geese, swerved from its course,
now graces with its temporary rest
our man-made pond, on which the last
light of the likewise migrant sun
has fallen.

follow him out of grace

Beyond the gate,
the yard slopes gently to the garden:
turnips, kale, one ancient tree
still bearing fruit.
Amid the unmown grass
about its roots, I can just see
the windfall apples, green and golden.

Out of grace, we bring forth children.

Catch

My father was holding a ball in the shape
of the sun. The sun,
he said, at four point five
billion years of age, is in its prime:
with more or less an equal span ahead
before, its hydrogen depleted,
it begins to slough its shells and eat
its children, a red
giant. By which time
you, my son, and I will be long gone, and all we love.
And then he tossed the ball to me. I didn't mean
to catch it but my hands reached up.

Refrain

Imagine it, Adam: old woman and grey,
I found myself walking again in the garden,
the trees in full fruit as they were on that day.
Therein lies the question: again, did I eat?
Again. It was as we remembered. More sweet.

JOURNEYWORK

Front Story

Phemios

At the end of the *Odyssey,* the *Iliad*
   comes back in all its terrible

   detail: Odysseus slaughtering
   suitors till the floor runs red

as great Scamandros; or 'rutting',
   lustful, 'in his rooted bed'.

   I didn't want to tell you,
but I have to since he spared me.

Islands

It was only after we had been
at sea for many days without
a sign of shore (unfriendly winds
had blown us far off course and we
despaired of finding Ithaca)
that I began to have the dream
of islands.

Waking – or I thought I woke –
I found myself at the centre of
an island large enough the sound
of breakers didn't penetrate
to where I stood. As if once more
bound fast to the mainmast of my ship,
I listened.

I heard the dry wind thrashing in
the branches of an olive tree;
the litter shifting where a snake
withdrew itself; a bird repeating
one high note (though whether to chide
his foes or warn his mate, I couldn't
tell you) –

but all these sounds, without the sea,
a recitation without the lyre,
afforded me, at last, no clew:
no sense of where to turn my feet
to find my way to the coast, and you.
It struck me it was possible I
was dreaming:

no sooner did the thought occur
than I woke again – or thought I woke –
and found myself again at the heart
of another island like the first.
Again I found myself restrained
by indecision, hawser-strong,
and woke

again, to the heart of another island.
Penelope, I could relate
no end of this: all night I woke,
to island after island, each one
blossoming within the last,
like rings around a boat at rest.
But dawn

did come. I woke indeed. I found
myself in my hollow ship. I almost
wept with joy to see the sea.

The Ship Examined

a whale

If I roll to port,
I sight it in my starboard eye.
They say the timber snout that furrows up our under-sky
is but the tip, so to speak, of the iceberg.

Our supra-tidal scout,
a gull, but disinclined to lie,
rehearses wonders:
a kind of reef, above, rigged out
in kelp-like cords; homunculi;
a row of brine-encrusted ports;
and pilings heaven-anchored.
                                        I
have heard the Labrador report
the calving of a glacier continents
away and, having seen great bergs
displacing fjords-worth of water,
shouldering their southwards way
from Paamiut to Providence,
reserve my judgment.

Dozing fifty fathoms deep,
I've watched their grave, diminishing procession:
upside-down basilicas. Or – *yan, tan,
tethera, pethera* – sheep.

Penelope in Heavy Weather

I feel that I could weather death
if only I could tell you of it after.

It's amazing what we've made all right
across this kitchen table. But how

could I relate, beyond the stopping
of the blood, the breath, the stopping

of relation? That's no country. Perhaps,
she said, taking up her glass – lifting

her glass of sea-dark wine – that's why
I spend such time telling you of it now.

Seadog on Ithaca

I cannot vouch for woven boats.
They'll do to carry babes downstream
to strange encampments – but give me
good tar and timber. So I told her.
Still I see her lantern, nights.
Awake by its loom light she sits
and caulks the seams of her tapestry.

Penelope Dreams of Geese

After a storm the ocean gathers
up its broken waves. A lifeguard,
my vocation is to save
lives – but no life is saved,
though my seat is made of olive wood
well seasoned and the timbers square,
the uprights plumb, the horizontals level.

Far inland where a grove of trees
affords good shelter from the wind,
the censure of the Ithacans,
I pledged myself to Aphrodite,
goddess of love and voyages,
the one who lets you save one life
at the expense of all the others.

Last night I dreamed a quick brown fox
had tunnelled under the courtyard wall
and one by one slain all my geese:
the white ones with their craning beaks;
the mottled, knobbly-headed one;
the little one who always followed
along behind; the masked one, and her mate.

The Girls

Busy in our wake the sea unravels
our wake. They say there are three Fates:
Clotho, who spins the thread of a man's
life, Lachesis, who draws it out,
and Atropos, who cuts it. What do they call
the one who simply follows along
behind, unravelling what her sisters have perplexed?
Surely she's most powerful of all.

At Dorion, the Muses, encountering
Thamyris, the boastful singer,
in their anger struck him maimed,
left him his voice but took away
his memory: a dreadful fate.
But wind and swell are Thamyris,
water falling on the water, scuffle
of gravel high on a seaside cliff.

When the wind is fair the sailors say
the girls are pulling with both hands.
They mean the girls at home, who hold
the rope that is, by long tradition,
thought to be made fast to our bows.
You who hold the linen cord
that's fastened to my stern, do you
remember all the patterns you unravel?

Wayfarer

At Ithaca
my waves begin,
who juggle sand,
who gather in
the wrack of land
and cast it up
upon the sea.
This is no common
tapestry.
I weave them gold
and green and grey
to the horizon
where they break.
I ravel in
the shuttle's wake.
And each day's labour's
lost, they say.
They do not see
how, slowly, the
horizon line
is worn away.
Some even tide
the night will fail
(it is but weft)
and day reveal
my landfall: as
you know, your sail.

Lookout

I watched the women hanging up the wash and thought, a single line
strung taut: the simplest tapestry.

Horizon, sky above and sea below: for twenty years I've known
no other story. Trouble is,

no sooner do you get down to the wire,
someone plucks it and begins, *Tell me, Muse, of the man of many ways* ...

for a single line is also the simplest lyre.

Back Story

Cassandra

You let that damned horse in again,
and history begins, again.
The story flashes in the pan:
the ship that launched a thousand men ...

The horse will bear, the cock will crow.
The rubes will interrupt the show.
The show goes on, for all we know.
The story goes, I told you so.

What the Sirens Said

Come closer and I'll tell you.

Odysseus on Watch

All night we tacked
against a head
wind. Moon breaking
up on the chop.

Impossible
to say if we
gained ground, they say,
even at sea.

I thought about
your hands, passing
the shuttle back
and forth: tacking.

Against what? O-
ther head winds, I
supposed. I won-
dered what you'd make

of our boustro-
phedonic pro-
gress, what if a-
nything did I.

Argos

When you returned the goddess hid
your island in a veil of mist:
the penetrating roads, the harbours
where all could anchor, the rocks going
straight up and the trees tall growing.
You smelled it out. You think I wouldn't
know you through your rags?

Every mongrel has a tale
to tell of ending. What I mean,
O traveller, O raconteur, O fortunate
Odysseus: it isn't the arrival,
it's the recognition scene.

You Are So Strange

You are so strange, you said. I thought you meant
the years had been unkind – and yes, I bridled
at that statement, thinking: time and tide
will do that to a person. If you've come to count
my grey hairs you can set your sail
right now and ask your goddess for a following
wind to take you back to Circe's island,
or evil, not-to-be-mentioned Ilion.

It wasn't until you said the words again
that I remembered other kinds of change:
before our tasks were emblems of our troubles
we used to plunge ourselves in the routine,
and, surfacing, find each other rich and strange.

Love, let us leave these logbooks, these tide tables.

Translations

You don't have to go far inland, these days, to have
your oar mistaken for a winnow-fan, your grapnel for a crook –
but then, you've never had to go far out to sea
to have your bones mistaken for coral, your eyes for pearls:
the sea is always the land, the land the sea translating,
into imperfect argots, into argol, *Argos,* argosies;
argling the meaning of 'ex halos' till the sun goes down
and all the journeying ways are darkened, until the ship
goes down and all hands babble of green fields. Inland,
Odysseus comes to grapnel in his father's vineyard. Planting
his oar among the vines, he tells Laertes of his quest.
A woman offered me a calix (or was it a conch shell?
a coracle?), one draught from which would make a man
seem other than he was. My dear companions, pigs!
With the heads and voices and bristles of pigs. I thought them none
the worse for that. Laertes trowels among his plants.
Ah. In the pearl of the beholder. What became
of the calix, then? Odysseus says, That vessel broke
and all the journeying ways were darkened. As they talk,
the sun goes down. The sun goes down; all hands are lost;
Odysseus takes up his winnow-fan and babbles of green swells.

Vessel

Bilingual vessel,
late Archaic;
a woman the colour
of clay looks out
across the vessel's
sintered black:

in all that dark water, never a bright sail.

Au verso, this
same woman, now
in silhouette,
looks out across
the vessel's ground,
unsintered red:

in all that bright water, never a black ship.

Pour out the water.
From the vantage
of the vase painter,
the distant traveller,
this momentary column
holds you up.

Envoi

I've been walking inland
for a long time,

friend:

when I hold up this oar,
what do you see?

ACKNOWLEDGEMENTS

I am grateful to my family and friends, without whose support I could not have made this work; to my editors and publisher; to the Ontario Arts Council and the Canada Council for the Arts.

My reading of the *Iliad* and the *Odyssey* I owe to Richmond Lattimore, whose translations are warp to the weft of *Journeywork*.

Poems from this book have appeared previously in the anthology *Undercurrents: New Voices in Canadian Poetry*, edited by Robyn Sarah (Cormorant Books, 2011), as well as in the following magazines and on-line journals: *Arc Poetry Magazine, The Bow-Wow Shop, Canadian Notes & Queries, Ephemeris, Newpoetry, The New Quarterly, Numéro Cinq,* and *Poetry*.

Three of these poems had their first appearance in letterpress keepsakes that John Haney and I produced, in small editions, under our imprint Daubers Press. I am grateful to John for permission to use a detail from his photograph *Island 94* on the cover of this book, for the four wood engravings that appear within its pages, and for much else.

Amanda Jernigan has published widely as a poet and essayist, and has written for the stage. *Groundwork: poems* is her first book. She lives in Canada with her husband, the artist John Haney.

Photograph by John Haney